OVERCOMING
Self-Sabotage

11 STORIES ON HOW TO GET RID OF DESTRUCTIVE HABITS

Hanna Olivas and Adriana Luna Carlos
Along with 9 Inspired Women Authors

Published by She Rises Studios Publishing **www.SheRisesStudios.com**.

ISBN: 978-1-960136-08-4

Table of Contents

INTRODUCTION

She Rises Studios was created and inspired by the mother-daughter duo Hanna Olivas and Adriana Luna Carlos. In the middle of 2020, when the world was at one of its most vulnerable times, we saw the need to embrace women globally by offering inspirational quotes, blogs, and articles. Then, in March of 2021, we launched our very own Women's Empowerment Podcast: ***She Rises Studios Podcast.***

It is now one of the most sought out Women based podcasts both nationally and internationally. You can find us on your favorite podcast platforms, such as Spotify, Google Podcasts, Apple Podcasts, IHeartRadio, and much more! We didn't stop there. Establishing a safe space for women has become an even deeper need. Due to a global pandemic, women lost their businesses, employment, homes, finances, spouses, and more.

We decided to form the She Rises Studios Community Facebook Group. An environment strictly for women about women. Our focus in this group is to educate and celebrate women globally. To meet them exactly where they are on their journey.

It's a group of Ordinary Women Doing EXTRAordinary Things.

As we continued to grow our network, we saw a need to help shape the minds and influences of women struggling with insecurities, doubts, fears, etc. From this, we created a global movement known as:

Overcoming Self-Sabotage

Become your own BIGGEST fan!

If you have ever felt held back from achieving your goals, then Overcoming Self Sabotage is the book for you! This book shows readers how to overcome the mental and emotional blocks that keep them from reaching their full potential.

Self sabotage is something that many people struggle with in life. It's the act of purposely holding yourself back from achieving goals or being successful. It can be caused by low self-esteem, fear of failure, or lack of confidence. The cycle can seem never ending if left unchecked; however, it doesn't have to be that way.

We believe all women deserve confidence and a healthy self-esteem.

This book will give you the tools to develop just that!

This book is an essential read for anyone who wants to release themselves from limiting beliefs and reach their fullest potential in life. With its down-to-earth advice and easy-to-understand strategies, Overcoming Self Sabotage will show you how to become your own ally rather than your own enemy – so you can finally achieve those goals!

She Rises Studios offers:

- She Rises Studios Publishing
- She Rises Studios Public Relations
- She Rises Studios Podcast
- She Rises Studios Magazine
- Becoming An Unstoppable Woman TV Show
- She Rises Studios Community
- She Rises Studios Academy

We won't stop encouraging women to be Unstoppable. This is just the beginning of our global movement.

She Rises, She Leads, She Lives...

With Love,
HANNA OLIVAS
ADRIANA LUNA CARLOS
SHE RISES STUDIOS
www.sherisesstudios.com

Hanna Olivas

Founder & CEO of She Rises Studios
Podcast & TV Host | Best Selling Author | Influential Speaker |
Blood Cancer Advocate | #BAUW Movement Creator

https://www.linkedin.com/company/she-rises-studios/
https://www.instagram.com/sherisesstudios
https://www.facebook.com/sherisesstudios
www.SheRisesStudios.com

Author, Speaker, and Founder. Hanna was born and raised in Las Vegas, Nevada, and has paved her way to becoming one of the most influential women of 2022. Hanna is the co-founder of She Rises Studios and the founder of the Brave & Beautiful Blood Cancer Foundation. Her journey started in 2017 when she was first diagnosed with Multiple Myeloma, an incurable blood cancer. Now more than ever, her focus is to empower other women to become leaders because The Future is Female. She is currently traveling and speaking publicly to women to educate them on entrepreneurship, leadership, and owning the female power within.

UNDERSTANDING SELF-SABOTAGE AND HOW IT HOLDS YOU BACK

By Hanna Olivas

I have always wanted to be a successful businesswoman, running my successful multi-digital media firm for women entrepreneurs. I was confident, ambitious, and driven, which showed in everything I did. But deep down, I have always battled a hidden enemy that threatened to derail everything I worked so hard to achieve: self-sabotage.

Self-sabotage is a common problem that affects many people and can take many forms. For me, it has been a constant nagging voice in my head that tells me I'm never going to be good enough, that I don't deserve success, and that I was destined to fail. I often set ambitious goals for myself, only to sabotage my efforts through procrastination, self-doubt, and negative self-talk.

My self-sabotage became a serious problem when I was approached by a potential client who wanted me to take on her large project. It was a high-profile opportunity that would have been a significant coup for my business, but as soon as I received the proposal, I felt a sense of dread wash over me. I began to question whether I could deliver the project, had the expertise and resources to handle it, and could manage the pressure and stress that would come with it.

As the days went by, I became increasingly anxious and overwhelmed, and I found myself procrastinating and avoiding the work that needed to be done. I started missing deadlines and failing to follow through on my commitments, and my confidence crumbled. I knew that if I didn't get a handle on my self-sabotage, I would lose the client and risk damaging her reputation.

Fortunately, I realized that I needed help and sought a therapist specializing in helping people overcome self-sabotage. Through a series of sessions, I began uncovering the underlying beliefs and fears driving my self-destructive behavior. I learned to recognize the negative self-talk and challenge the limiting beliefs holding me back.

One of the key insights I gained from therapy was that I was suffering from impostor syndrome, a psychological phenomenon in which a person doubts their abilities and feels like a fraud, even in the face of evidence of the contrary. I realized that I had been telling myself a story that I was not good enough, was not worthy of success, and was only succeeding because of luck or other external factors. This story had been holding me back for years, and it was time to rewrite it.

I began to practice self-compassion and self-forgiveness, learning to be kind to myself and let go of past mistakes and failures. I started to focus on my strengths and accomplishments rather than dwelling on my shortcomings and failures. I learned to set realistic goals for myself and to celebrate her progress along the way.

As I continued to work on myself, I found that my self-sabotage dissipated. I started to take on more challenging projects with confidence and enthusiasm, and I could deliver exceptional results. I no longer felt like a fraud but rather like a competent, capable professional who was worthy of success.

Today, my business is thriving, and I have a reputation as a skilled and reliable expert in my field. I have learned to recognize and overcome myself-sabotage, and I am now passionate about helping others do the same. I speak at conferences and events, sharing my story and insights with others struggling with self-doubt and negative self-talk.

In conclusion, self-sabotage can be a debilitating problem that can prevent people from achieving their full potential. However, it is possible to overcome it with the right tools and support.

Self-sabotage can take many forms, including procrastination, negative self-talk, and self-doubt. Overcoming self-sabotage requires a combination of self-awareness, self-compassion, and practical strategies. Here are 15 ways to overcome self-sabotage:

1. Identify your self-sabotaging behaviors: Start by becoming aware of the behaviors that are holding you back. Take note of when you procrastinate, make excuses, or engage in negative self-talk.

2. Recognize your triggers: Identify the situations, people, or emotions that trigger your self-sabotage. This can help you anticipate and prepare for these situations in the future.

3. Practice self-compassion: Be kind to yourself, especially when you make mistakes or fail. Avoid harsh self-criticism; instead, focus on learning from your experiences and improving for the future.

4. Challenge limiting beliefs: Identify the limiting beliefs that underlie your self-sabotage. These might include beliefs like "I'm not good enough" or "I don't deserve success." Challenge these beliefs with evidence to the contrary.

5. Set realistic goals: Set achievable goals for yourself rather than setting unrealistic expectations that set you up for failure.

6. Focus on progress, not perfection: Instead of focusing on achieving perfection, focus on making progress toward your goals. Celebrate your small successes along the way.

7. Break down large goals into smaller tasks: Break down large projects into smaller, more manageable tasks. This can help you avoid feeling overwhelmed and make the project more achievable.

8. Practice mindfulness: Mindfulness can help you stay present and focused, which can prevent you from getting distracted or overwhelmed by negative thoughts.

9. Surround yourself with positive influences: Surround yourself with people who uplift and support you rather than those who bring you down or encourage your self-sabotaging behaviors.
10. Take care of your physical and mental health: Prioritize your physical and mental health by getting enough sleep, exercise, and healthy food. This can help you feel more energized and motivated.
11. Get help: Don't be afraid to ask for help when you need it. This could include seeking support from friends or family or reaching out to a therapist or coach.
12. Visualize success: Visualize yourself succeeding in your goals, and imagine how it will feel when you achieve them. This can motivate you and keep you focused on positive outcomes.
13. Practice gratitude: Focus on the things in your life that you are grateful for rather than dwelling on the negative. This can help shift your perspective and improve your mood.
14. Take action: Instead of waiting for motivation or inspiration to strike, take action toward your goals. Even small steps can help build momentum and increase your confidence.
15. Practice self-care: Take time for yourself to do the things that make you happy and recharge your batteries. This can help you feel more balanced and prevent burnout.

Love, faith, and forgiveness can be powerful tools in overcoming self-sabotage. Here's how each one can help:

- Love: Love can help you overcome self-sabotage by providing a sense of motivation and purpose. When you love yourself and are motivated by love, you are more likely to care for yourself, set realistic goals, and prioritize self-improvement. Love can also help you be kinder to yourself when you make mistakes, which can prevent negative self-talk and self-sabotaging behaviors.

- Faith: Faith can help you overcome self-sabotage by providing a sense of hope and trust in a higher power or greater purpose. When you have faith, you may feel less burdened by your own limitations and more confident in your ability to overcome obstacles. Faith can also provide a sense of accountability and responsibility, encouraging you to take action toward your goals and strive for personal growth.
- Forgiveness: Forgiveness can help you overcome self-sabotage by allowing you to let go of past mistakes and move forward with a sense of peace and self-acceptance. When you forgive yourself for past mistakes, you are less likely to dwell on them and more likely to focus on the present and future. Forgiveness can also help you avoid self-destructive behaviors that are rooted in feelings of shame or guilt.

Together, love, faith, and forgiveness can provide a powerful foundation for overcoming self-sabotage. When you approach yourself and your goals with love and self-compassion, trust in a greater purpose or power, and a willingness to forgive yourself for past mistakes, you can break free from self-sabotaging behaviors and achieve greater success and fulfillment in your life.

When you are free from self-sabotage and limiting beliefs, you open yourself up to a world of new possibilities and opportunities. Here are some of the positive outcomes you might experience:

1. Increased self-confidence: When you no longer hold yourself back with self-sabotaging behaviors or limiting beliefs, you are free to pursue your goals with greater self-confidence and self-assurance.

2. Improved relationships: Self-sabotage can often manifest in relationships, causing you to push people away or engage in negative patterns. When you are free from self-sabotage, your relationships improve as you are more open and receptive to positive connections with others.
3. Greater success: Limiting beliefs and self-sabotaging behaviors can hold you back from achieving your full potential. When you break free from these patterns, you are able to achieve greater success in your personal and professional life.
4. More fulfilling experiences: Self-sabotage can prevent you from fully experiencing life, as you may hold yourself back from new experiences or opportunities. When you are free from self-sabotage, you can fully embrace new experiences and find more fulfillment in your life.
5. Improved mental health: Self-sabotage can be rooted in negative self-talk and self-criticism, which can lead to anxiety, depression, and other mental health issues. When you break free from these patterns, you may find that your mental health improves as you are more positive and self-affirming.

Overall, being free from self-sabotage and limiting beliefs can help you live a more fulfilling and authentic life that is not hindered by negative patterns or beliefs. It can help you achieve greater success, form deeper connections with others, and experience more joy and fulfillment in your life.

Helping others overcome self-sabotage can be a delicate process, but here are some general tips to keep in mind:

1. Practice active listening: When someone is struggling with self-sabotage, it's important to listen to their concerns and validate their experiences. Practice active listening by giving them your full attention, asking open-ended questions, and reflecting

back on what you've heard to ensure you understand their perspective.

2. Encourage self-compassion: Self-compassion can be a powerful tool in overcoming self-sabotage. Encourage your loved one to practice self-compassion by being kind to themselves, recognizing their own limitations, and reframing negative self-talk.

3. Help them identify patterns: Often, self-sabotage is rooted in negative thinking or behavior patterns. Help your loved one identify these patterns by asking them to reflect on past experiences and looking for common themes or triggers.

4. Offer support: Let your loved one know that you are there for them and offer your support in whatever way they need. This might mean providing a listening ear, helping them set achievable goals, or providing resources for therapy or counseling.

5. Be patient and non-judgmental: Overcoming self-sabotage can be a long and challenging process, and it's important to be patient and non-judgmental as your loved one works through it. Avoid blaming or criticizing their progress; instead, focus on offering support and encouragement.

Remember that everyone's journey to overcoming self-sabotage is unique, and what works for one person may not work for another. By being patient, empathetic, and supportive, you can help your loved one find their own path toward self-growth and personal success.

Gratitude can be a powerful tool in overcoming self-sabotage. Here are some ways that practicing gratitude can help:

1. Shifts focus from negative to positive: Focusing on things you're grateful for can shift your attention away from negative thoughts or self-sabotaging behaviors. This can help break the

cycle of negative thinking and allow you to see the positive aspects of your life.

2. Increases self-awareness: Practicing gratitude can help you become more aware of your thoughts and behaviors. When you actively seek out things to be grateful for, it can help you recognize how you may be holding yourself back with self-sabotage.

3. Promotes self-acceptance: Gratitude can help you accept yourself for who you are, flaws, and all. This can help you avoid self-destructive behaviors that are rooted in negative self-talk or self-criticism.

4. Encourages positive self-talk: When you practice gratitude, you are more likely to engage in positive self-talk, which can help combat negative self-talk and self-sabotage.

5. Boosts mood and resilience: Gratitude has been shown to boost mood and resilience, which can help you stay motivated and focused on your goals, even in the face of setbacks or obstacles.

To incorporate gratitude into your life, consider starting a gratitude journal, where you write down things you're grateful for each day. You can also make a habit of expressing gratitude to others, whether it's through a thank you note, a phone call, or a simple compliment. By practicing gratitude regularly, you can help break free from self-sabotage and live a more fulfilling, positive life.

Self-sabotaging thoughts can have a negative impact on the body, both physically and mentally. Here are some examples:

1. Chronic stress: Self-sabotaging thoughts can cause chronic stress, which can lead to a variety of physical health problems, such as high blood pressure, heart disease, and digestive issues.

2. Weakened immune system: Prolonged stress from self-sabotaging thoughts can also weaken the immune system, making you more susceptible to illnesses and infections.
3. Mental health issues: Self-sabotage can lead to anxiety, depression, and other mental health issues, which can further impact physical health.
4. Poor sleep: Self-sabotaging thoughts can interfere with sleep, leading to fatigue and a weakened immune system.
5. Unhealthy coping mechanisms: In an effort to cope with self-sabotaging thoughts and emotions, people may turn to unhealthy coping mechanisms such as alcohol or drug abuse, overeating, or other forms of self-harm, which can have long-term negative effects on the body.

It's important to address self-sabotaging thoughts and behaviors in order to reduce the negative impact on the body. This may include seeking therapy, practicing self-care, and developing healthier coping mechanisms. By addressing self-sabotage, individuals can improve their overall health and well-being.

Ditching self-sabotage can be key to achieving success in life and business. Here are some ways in which overcoming self-sabotage can help you attain success:

1. Clearer vision and goals: When you let go of self-sabotaging thoughts and behaviors, you can gain clarity around your goals and vision for your life or business. This can help you stay focused and motivated and make decisions that align with your values and aspirations.
2. Improved self-confidence: Overcoming self-sabotage can help you develop a stronger sense of self-confidence, which can help

you take risks and pursue new opportunities. This can be especially important in business, where self-confidence can be key to networking, pitching ideas, and closing deals.

3. Better relationships: Self-sabotage can impact your thoughts and behaviors and your relationships with others. By overcoming self-sabotage, you can develop healthier, more supportive relationships that can help you succeed in both life and business.
4. Greater resilience: Overcoming self-sabotage can help you develop greater resilience in the face of challenges or setbacks. This can be especially important in business, where failure is often part of the process. By learning to bounce back from setbacks, you can stay focused on your goals and keep moving forward.
5. Increased productivity: Self-sabotage can be a major roadblock to productivity, as it can lead to procrastination, indecision, and lack of motivation. By overcoming self-sabotage, you can become more productive and efficient in your personal and professional life.

Overcoming self-sabotage can help you succeed in life and business by providing greater clarity, confidence, resilience, and productivity. Recognizing and addressing self-sabotaging thoughts and behaviors can unlock your full potential and help you reach your goals. I hope and pray you drop those limiting beliefs and self-sabotaging habits once and for all and live your life without limits!

Xoxo,
Hanna Olivas

Adriana Luna Carlos

Founder and CEO of She Rises Studios & FENIX TV

https://www.linkedin.com/in/adriana-luna-carlos/
https://www.facebook.com/adrianalunacarlos
https://www.instagram.com/sherisesstudios/
https://www.sherisesstudios.com/
https://www.srslatina.com/
https://fenixtv.app/

Adriana Luna Carlos is an accomplished web and graphic designer, author, and mentor with a passion for helping women succeed in life and business. With over 10 years of experience in graphic and web arts, Adriana has built a reputation as an innovative leader and entrepreneur. In 2020, she co-founded She Rises Studios, a multi-digital media company and publishing house that has helped countless clients achieve their branding and marketing goals. In 2023, she co-created FENIX TV, an online streaming platform that showcases stories of people breaking barriers, shattering stereotypes, and triumphing against the odds.

As an advocate for women's success, Adriana challenges her clients and mentees to strive for nothing less than excellence. She has a deep understanding of the insecurities and challenges that women often face in the business world and provides the guidance and resources needed to overcome them. Her success as a business leader and entrepreneur has made her a sought-after mentor and speaker at events around the world.

Through her work, Adriana has demonstrated a commitment to creating opportunities for women to succeed in business and life. Her passion for innovation, leadership, and women's empowerment has made her a respected figure in the business community, and her impact will undoubtedly continue to inspire and empower women for years to come.

MY JOURNEY TO SELF-AWARENESS AND EMPOWERMENT

By Adriana Luna Carlos

At first, I didn't even realize I was doing it. Whenever I set a goal or had a dream, I would find a way to sabotage myself. Whether procrastinating, making excuses, or engaging in self-destructive behaviors, I always managed to undermine my success.

It was like a subconscious pattern repeating itself, no matter how hard I tried to break free from it. I would start with enthusiasm and determination, but soon enough, I would lose momentum and fall back into my old ways.

So, I decided to step back and examine my behavior patterns. I started journaling and identifying why I did what I did. I realized my self-sabotage was rooted in deep-seated beliefs about myself and my abilities. I had internalized many negative messages from my past experiences, and I had come to believe that I was not worthy of the success I had envisioned for myself.

Once I became aware of these beliefs, I could challenge them and replace them with more positive and empowering ones. I started practicing self-compassion and self-care and learned to celebrate my successes instead of dwelling on my failures. I also started setting realistic goals and breaking them down into manageable steps to make progress without feeling overwhelmed.

Of course, overcoming self-sabotage is not a linear process. Sometimes I would slip back into my old ways, but I learned to forgive myself and keep moving forward. I also reached out to friends and loved ones for support, and I found that sharing my struggles with others helped me feel less alone and more accountable.

Self-sabotage is a behavior that stops us from achieving our goals and living our best lives. It's an insidious phenomenon that can take many forms and be difficult to recognize in ourselves, leaving us feeling overwhelmed and helpless. In this chapter, we will look at what self-sabotage is, who can struggle with it, and how to overcome it.

Self-sabotage refers to the behaviors and thought patterns that prevent us from achieving our goals and reaching our full potential. It can take many forms, such as procrastination, self-doubt, negative self-talk, self-destructive behavior, or even intentionally undermining oneself.

Anyone can experience self-sabotaging behavior—not limited to any gender identity or age group. We may be more likely to engage in self-sabotaging behavior if we have low self-esteem or are dealing with anxiety or depression. We may also engage in destructive habits if we feel like there's no way out of a situation (i.e., feeling trapped) or want revenge against someone who has wronged us but doesn't want them directly implicated in the outcome (i.e., indirect revenge).

There are many reasons why people engage in self-sabotaging behaviors. Here are just a few:

1. Fear of failure: Many people sabotage themselves because they fear failing or not meeting their or others' expectations. They may feel like they are incapable or worthy of success, and as a result, they engage in behaviors that prevent them from trying or fully committing to their goals.

2. Fear of success: On the other hand, some people may sabotage themselves because they fear what success might bring. They may worry about the added pressure or responsibility that comes with success or fear they will lose their sense of identity or connection to others if they succeed.

3. Low self-esteem: People with low self-esteem may sabotage

themselves because they don't believe they are capable or deserving of success. They may have internalized negative messages from their past experiences or relationships, so they struggle to see themselves in a positive light.

4. Perfectionism: Perfectionists may sabotage themselves because they are so focused on achieving a perfect outcome that they become overwhelmed or paralyzed by their high standards. They may procrastinate or feel self-doubt because they feel like they can't meet their expectations.

Regardless of the reasons behind self-sabotage, there are several ways to overcome it:

1. Increase self-awareness: The first step in overcoming self-sabotage is to become aware of the behaviors and thought patterns holding you back. Take time to reflect on your goals and the obstacles you have faced in achieving them. Consider keeping a journal or seeking therapy to help you gain deeper insights into your behavior.

2. Challenge negative beliefs: Once you have identified the beliefs contributing to your self-sabotage, challenge them. Ask yourself if they are true or based on old or outdated information. Replace negative self-talk with positive affirmations and remind yourself of your strengths and past successes.

3. Take small steps: It can be overwhelming to try to tackle a big goal all at once. Instead, break your goal down into smaller, more manageable steps. Celebrate your progress along the way and use your successes to build momentum.

4. Practice self-compassion: Be kind to yourself and acknowledge that setbacks and mistakes are a normal part of learning. Treat

yourself with the same kindness and compassion you would offer a struggling friend.

5. Seek support: Don't be afraid to reach out to friends, family, or a therapist for support. Talking to others can help you gain perspective and feel less alone. It can also provide you with accountability and encouragement to keep going.

Through all this learning, studying, and introspection over time, my confidence grew exponentially, which allowed me the emotional courage to take risks when previously I wouldn't have had the guts to - like applying for jobs outside of my comfort zone or starting my own business ventures! These experiences have also helped build an even deeper understanding of who I am by showing me what works best for ME - not anyone else!

One of the most important aspects of becoming empowered is having an unshakeable belief in yourself - no matter what life throws at you! This is something that took time but eventually became natural through continued practice, such as journaling daily affirmations or repeating mantras each morning. And now, here we are today!

If you are struggling with self-sabotage, I encourage you to take a similar approach. Start by examining your behavior patterns and identifying the beliefs holding you back. Then, challenge those beliefs and replace them with more positive ones. Practice self-compassion and self-care, and reach out to others for support when you need it. Remember, you are capable of overcoming your self-sabotage and achieving your goals.

My journey is still ongoing, but it has already given me a greater sense of clarity about what matters most in life: taking care of yourself first so you can take care of others too; setting boundaries; embracing imperfection; being kinder towards yourself; having difficult conversations; all while having faith that you will get where you need to go if you keep moving forward one step at a time. The people you surround yourself with can either support or hinder your progress. Surround yourself with positive and supportive people who encourage and motivate you.

Self-sabotage can seem like an insurmountable obstacle, but luckily, there are strategies available which allow us to take back control over our lives! By becoming mindful of how these behaviors manifest themselves, setting achievable goals, and getting support from those around us - we can overcome whatever obstacles come our way!

Cindy Witteman

Founder/CEO of Driving Single Parents Inc

https://www.linkedin.com/in/cindy-witteman-a48851253
https://www.facebook.com/profile.php?id=100089195777362&mibextid=LQQJ4d
www.instagram.com/cindy.witteman
www.DrivingSingleParents.org
www.CFViews.com

My Name is Cindy Witteman, I live in San Antonio Texas. I am a Business Owner, Author, Non-Profit Startup Coach, Host of "Little Give" TV Show and Founder/CEO of Driving Single Parents Inc. I am a former single parent and proud step mom with a total of 6 kids, and 3 grandchildren. I love to travel, spend time with family, and am a pilot in progress. I have a passion for giving back and helping single parents regain their independence. Driving Single Parents, a 501(c)3 Non-Profit which just celebrated 6 years in existence. We have successfully changed the lives of multiple single parent families with reliable vehicles, at NO cost to them. These parents have gone on to have success stories of their own by using the car as a tool. The vehicles have given them the ability to transform their single parent struggles into a thing of the past.

HOW TO OVERCOME SELF-SABOTAGE

By Cindy Witteman

"Whether you think you can,
or you think you can't –
you're right." – Henry Ford

If I were to list all the times I had to change my train of thought to stop self-sabotaging, I would run out of space in this book.

In grade school, I kept myself out of the spotlight due to my tremendous fear of being ridiculed. After all, I was already convinced that I was too skinny and awkward. I didn't want anyone else to notice all of my flaws. Therefore, I would avoid reading aloud in class, volunteering to work in group settings, or doing anything else that might draw attention.

As a child, we struggled with low income, meaning we went without many basic necessities that most people take for granted. This caused me to be self-conscious and forced me to deal with adult problems that most kids never even know exist. I constantly felt judged and was bullied all throughout my childhood for being poor and not very well-spoken. Thus further reinforcing my need to hide in the shadows and never explore my true potential.

In my early teens, a group of friends begged me to join the school cheerleading team. But in my mind, there was absolutely NO WAY I could overcome my fear of being seen enough to join. Therefore, I opted to become the High School Mascot. It was perfect because I could enjoy all of the fun of entertaining the crowd while being hidden behind my mask. Almost no one in the school knew I was the one in the bulldog costume all along. My ongoing internal struggles continued into my twenties. With a failed marriage and a divorce pending due to domestic violence, I was terrified of falling flat in all aspects of my life. I feared being inadequate as a mother, provider, daughter, or worst of all, being unsuccessful at my new role as a single mother. No matter how hard I had to work, I was not going to let that happen!

Although my mom had primary custody of me and raised me for most of my childhood, my dad played a key role in my life. I always admired him for his amazing storytelling abilities and strong work ethic. He was fantastic with money, had a good job, nice things, and a stable home life. One of the key pieces of advice he gave me that I still use in my everyday life is to always do the right thing. Anytime I would struggle with making a decision, he would tell me STOP and ask myself, "What's the right thing to do?" Then just DO THAT, even when it's hard.

When I was 26, I worked as a Sales Manager. My position required me to work weekends and holidays, and it had a minimum requirement of 50 hours per week. But in order to complete the duties, it took more like 55 or 60. My place of employment was also 40+ minutes from home. Spending all of this time away from my daughters was excruciating. However, I thought it was my only option at the time because I was their sole provider.

One day my dad told me I should consider changing my employment to something more stable with weekends and holidays off. Otherwise, my daughters were going to grow up without even knowing me. Taking this job would require me to take a HUGE pay cut and be in a completely different career field than what I was used to. My first fear was financial, and the second and most concerning was my own self-limiting beliefs. What if I wasn't smart enough and couldn't do the job? What if I failed and my employment was terminated? If I was terminated, how would I get back on my feet to support my daughters? I would not only let my dad down, but I feared becoming an embarrassment. Therefore, I almost didn't take the opportunity once it was offered. However, I knew if it was to be, it was up to me! So, with my dad's encouraging words and strong push for me to take the job, I reluctantly agreed. Now I have been working in the legal field for 15 years and couldn't be happier with that decision.

This just goes back to reinforce how my own thoughts and fears have almost held me back from exploring GREAT opportunities. I'm grateful that my dad had so much faith in me even when I didn't believe in myself. Otherwise, I would still be in a dead-end job working 50+ hours a week with no time to spend with my family and no opportunity to explore my own interests outside of work.

It wasn't until I was in my 30s that I realized how much my self-limiting beliefs were holding me back from accomplishing my goals and fulfilling my dreams. Once I had the realization, it was time to get to work!

At first, it was hard to believe that it was me who prevented myself from participating in programs at my daughter's school, that I turned down countless career advancements and several invitations to play on various work group sporting events. Self-doubt and negative thoughts alone kept me on the sidelines. Fear once again prevented me from enjoying life because I never allowed myself to win or lose because I never even tried.

Once I realized it was a ME problem…

My life finally began! I changed my thought patterns and started to work on myself. I spent the time learning what I wanted, set career goals, relationship standards, and made a plan to ensure my personal life flourished. It was then that I grew a voice, progressed in my career, stopped bad relationship cycles, picked a cause, and decided how I wanted to give back to this world.

When I decided to start Driving Single Parents Inc., I had all of the same fears I had in previous endeavors, but I made a vow to myself that I would push past the fear and go for it! With every step I took toward the start of the Non-Profit, I experienced self-doubt. At first, I thought it was simple. I found a solution that would provide this much needed resource to struggling single parents. How hard could it be? But once I started diving into it and realized how much went into not only starting a non-profit but growing it, that stream of self-doubt started to creep back in. Can I really do this? Will anyone else think this is a good cause that will actually help? With all that negativity swirling around in my head, I remembered to push through the fear and follow my heart. My heart was telling me this was an amazing, much needed organization that would be a total game changer for single parents working their butts off, trying to make a good life for their families.

According to the Federal Reserve Economic Data, approximately 35% of Bexar County residents live in a single parent home.

Once I had the data to reflect the need for a Non-Profit strictly focused on single-parent households, I knew it was time to strike while the iron was hot and the idea was fresh in my mind. Within 24 hours of having the idea to start a Non-Profit **focused on providing single parents with vehicles**, a plan was formulated, and the website was built. Taking action as soon as the idea became clear in my mind was SO important because I knew if I waited and didn't start right away, fear and my own self-limiting beliefs would have kept me from moving forward.

Soon enough, I had the footing in place and registered the name "Driving Single Parents, Inc." with the Secretary of State. The first car giveaway took place less than 20 days later. I purchased the first vehicle with my own hard-earned money, and the vehicle was given to an extremely deserving single dad. I intentionally picked out a Sport Utility Vehicle because he was involved in a motor vehicle accident caused by a drunk driver. In that accident, he not only lost his vehicle, but he also lost his wife, and his right leg had to be amputated due to the gravity of his injuries. After months of painstaking rehabilitation, he was ready to get back in the driver's seat, but lacked the ability to purchase his own vehicle due to lost time at work, extensive medical bills, and the need for a vehicle that could accommodate his children and handicap needs.

Shortly thereafter, I had several close friends and co-workers volunteer to help. My good friend and colleague Justin Clark jumped in and became a board member. Soon we had Brian Siller join us as the Treasurer & Jamie Mathis as our Secretary. Michael Ritter, Andrew Froelich, and Minerva Mendoza really helped us with our 501(c)3 Non-Profit designation with the IRS. This was just to name a few of the many people who believed in the cause and jumped on the board of directors to lend a helping hand.

Despite the positive reassurances I received from the community, I had to constantly push away the fear and stop myself from self-sabotaging on a daily basis. I ultimately had to tell myself once again to follow my heart, do it afraid, and it will all work out exactly how it's meant to.

One of the main things I struggled with was my fear of public speaking. In the beginning of this chapter, I mentioned how I became a master at staying behind the scenes and out of the spotlight. Well, with my new role as Founder and CEO, I was the face of the organization and was expected to do news interviews, podcasts, and speak about the organization at any given opportunity. It was a total nightmare at first! Not only did I have to do it, but I had to live with the fact that everyone I knew would see it. Every clip would put ME on display for the whole world to critique. However, once I got more comfortable, I realized that I was my own biggest critic. I would obsess over every missed step, awkward smile, nervous tic, and hair mishap. Friends and family members would reach out to tell me how wonderful I did. So many people told me that my interviews looked so natural, and I answered the questions with heart and excitement. It turns out that my own self-sabotaging thoughts caused all of my stress and anxiety. No one else even seemed to notice how I was totally out of my element during those interviews.

There is this one specific time I will never forget. It was the first big fundraiser for Driving Single Parents, Inc., and the local news came to report on our organization. I was SO thrilled they came to capture our efforts and share them with the world. This was BIG! The word was going to get out, which would undoubtedly help us grow. Well… when the camera guy started trying to mic me up—I panicked!

I tried to get anyone around me to do the interview in my place. Can somebody—ANYBODY—take my place and do the interview for me? They all told me, "NO, it will only be impactful if it comes straight from YOUR mouth. You are the Founder. Everyone is here because of you and your mission." Reluctantly, I gave the first interview—terrified—and every single one has gotten a little easier since.

Fast forward, and Driving Single Parents, Inc. just celebrated six years in existence and has changed the lives of multiple single parent families. If I hadn't put my little idea into action because I let fear rule me, Driving Single Parents would still be a little idea going nowhere, stuck in my mind forever. It's hard to believe that if I had not mastered the ability to push through the fear and do it afraid, this organization would not exist.

While speaking to people I admire, I realized they have the same doubts and fears as me. I've had mentors tell me that they think I have incredible speaking abilities and wish they could deliver an interview as effortlessly as I do. This information just blew my mind because I believed that they had the ability to deliver a speech flawlessly without any preparation. It turns out they were also experiencing self-doubt about their abilities. Despite their cool exterior, they also felt panicky while delivering speeches and experienced the same anxiety about public speaking. I think it all comes down to the idea that we are our own worst enemies. We constantly have that little voice in our heads telling us we can't.

When I was offered the opportunity to Host my own TV-Show, I immediately thought of all of the reasons why I couldn't, shouldn't, and wouldn't ever do that. However, once again, I pushed through the fear and reluctantly agreed. I went from being terrified of public speaking to hosting a TV-Show. How ironic is that? Being that the premise of this show is to highlight ordinary people doing extraordinary things to help others, and why even a Little Give can make a big impact, it just felt right, and I knew that it was worth doing it afraid once again.

So the next time you think about how the people you look up to are flawless… just remember that they probably have the same doubts you do!

All of us experience self-limiting beliefs and self-sabotage throughout our lives. It's interesting that we all seem to think we are the only ones living with these stressors that consistently hold us back and almost prevent us from fulfilling our dreams and experiencing our true potential.

One of the silliest things I would do when I was having a moment of self-doubt was to listen to a specific song. It's actually kind of funny to picture a grown woman in her car blaring "The Climb" by Miley Cyrus, but it really helped me get through some really tough times.

Without fear and self-doubt holding me back, I was able to start Driving Single Parents, Inc., a 501(c)3 Non-Profit, which continues to help single parent families regain their independence by providing them with a vehicle at NO COST to them. I became an International Best Selling Author, Business Owner, Non-Profit Startup Coach, The Host of the "Little Give" TV Show, and best of all, I have truly become an unstoppable woman!

You are capable of doing this much and more if you can master the art of pushing past the fear and doing it afraid.

Tamara Shields

Founder of Green Acres Brokerage, LLC

https://www.facebook.com/tamarashields2020
https://www.medicareenroll.com/?purl=XiE09fog

Tamara Shields is the founder of Green Acres Brokerage, the mother of four boys, and serves in leadership within her church community. She devotes most of her time providing affordable health insurance and education to our communities. Tamara is dedicated to assisting Medicare and non-Medicare beneficiaries with obtaining the benefits they're entitled to. If the complications of insurance makes you want to pull your hair out, she can help stir you in the right direction. She's also a believer in community outreach and supports our communities by providing laundry detergent at laundromats to those in need, and food pantries for those who suffer from food insecurity. In her free time, you will find her singing and dancing around the house while preparing a home cooked meal.

BE CAREFUL WHAT YOU FEED IT MAY BE FEEDING OFF OF YOU

By Tamara Shields

There are two sides to each of us, and they originate from our heart's deepest, innermost meditations. Yes, they are found in the silence when there's no one else around and it's just you, spending intimate time with you. One is known as fear, and the other is faith, and they are both striving to thrive. There's no question that whichever side we choose to feed the most will dominate and influence our actions and greatly impact our results. They both desire to be fed several times daily to sustain longevity, and bring forth much fruit. For this reason, there's always a tug-of-war going on within us. They are both fighting to plead their case to win our attention because they know that we have the power to choose who we will allow to rise and take action.

Fear hassles us during the night, causing sleeplessness over the thoughts of not being good enough. It whispers in our ear, "What if you fail?" "What if you're not pretty enough?" "What if what they said about you is true?" "You should just give up now before you have too much invested." It cages our minds by telling us our ideas are far stretched and impossible to obtain. It closes our mouth by telling us we're not intellectual enough to make a difference. It binds the mistakes we've made in the past around our necks, leaving us gasping for peace. It ties our hands with a clenched fist, afraid that we will lose everything we have if we open ourselves up to new opportunities. After it's done dragging us by our feet through the puddle of nobody loves us, it wakes us up with a warm cup of tears to start the pity party.

Fear does not play fair. There are no boundaries that it will not cross to win our attention over faith. It's obsessed with our cry out for mercy as our voice reaches the peak of the highest mountain and our sorrow scrubs the floor of the lowest valley. It delights in the craftiness of our tongue's ability to speak doubt against ourselves and marvels at the sound of the most inventive curse words aimed at those who come to our rescue. Fear doesn't count calories; it consumes everything in its path. It wastes away our hopes and dreams, blurs any visions of us living up to our fullest potential, and burns off all our energy, leaving us physically and mentally exhausted. Then, it shows up the next day begging for a refill. Yes, it desires to feed off your emotions, starve you of your happiness, and dehydrate your ability to thrive.

While fear is persistent in convincing us to jump down the slippery slope of self-sabotage, faith pulls the other end of the rope screaming, "Take my hand, I'll pull you up!" Unlike fear, faith gives us peace during the night by encouraging us that everything will be just fine if we hold on. It whispers in our ear, "So what if you fail, I'll be there to dust you off, and you just try again," "You are beautifully and wonderfully made," "Who cares what they say about you? You know who you are and that's all that matters," "You can never invest too much when you're investing in yourself, you can do this." Instead of caging our mind, faith wrestles to set us free and encourages us to dream big because there's nothing too impossible for God.

It nudges us to enter rooms that others wouldn't dare and causes us to open our mouths to let inspiration flow, penetrating the hearts of men, women, boys, and girls. It refrains from binding our past mistakes around our neck; however, it gives us a friendly reminder to stay on course because we are trailblazers for those who are watching. With its sweet, gentle approach, it encourages us to open up the palm of our hand and be cheerful givers, meeting the needs of our neighbors to the best of our ability, knowing that God will not leave us begging for bread. Faith causes us to spring forth with gladness as we embark on new opportunities, with the understanding that God is in the mist. Unlike fear, it doesn't desire to drag us through the mud. However, faith walks us by still waters, causes fear to cease, and reminds us that we are loved. It greets us in the morning with a warm cup of God, as every inch of our body feels the tingling sensation of his goodness, and it's left us desiring a refill. Yes, faith also desires to be fed, it wants our heartaches and pains in exchange for unspeakable joy, and it hydrates our ability to thrive with living water flowing from above.

Faith nor fear have respect for persons. We will all experience waking up to them in the morning, seeing their faces throughout the day, and lying next to us during the night. No one can escape this crossroad of decision. I, too, am not exempt. As soon as I open my eyes in the morning, they both come rushing in. I'm left with a brief moment to decide whose side I'm on. Some days I'm persuaded to follow fear as all my imperfections are revealed to me. However, I manage not to stay there long because faith swiftly calls me back, reminding me that God did not give us the spirit of fear but of a sound mind. Then, I'm reminded that it's my imperfections that make me unique and keeps me humbled. Don't get me wrong, I spend time in the mirror examining myself just like the next person. I notice every scar, blemish, grey hair, and weight gain, but there's something even greater that I see. I see the love of God staring back at me. We all have battle wounds from life. Some are more visible than others, but they're present to let us know that we're living, and I, too, experience my share of trials and tribulations. I've survived a divorce and four boys, and trust me there were times I feared I wouldn't make it. It felt as if everyone I loved had a meeting and decided they would collaborate to take me down. The pain was as if my fingernails were being ripped out one by one, right along with my hair. I felt like giving up because I feared that no one loved me, but faith wrapped its arms around me. It reminded me that fear comes in all shapes and sizes and will do anything to cause you to self-destruct. Fear seeped its way in and caused me to feel under attack, but later, I discovered that it was nothing more than trials and tribulations that I was going through. I've also come to an understanding that everyone has their own journey to walk, even the people I love. Therefore, I stopped taking everything so personally and began to view everyone as people searching for their own path in life. It's faith that allows me to see the good within the bad and count it all as joy, knowing that the good and the bad are working together for my good. Although there are still times when I don't understand why certain things must be, the unknown is always unveiled with the beauty of a blessing. My journey has been bitter-sweet. The bitter is to let me know that I'm human and I'm not above anyone else, and the sweet lets me know that life is worth living.

Yes, fear and faith are waging war deep down within us daily, both laying all their cards on the table, pleading their case, awaiting the answer from the jury. You and I are the jury. We must decide who is telling the truth. Although they both have different motives, they must be fed to thrive. Who will you feed? Who will you give your time, energy, emotions, dreams, and visions? Will you side with fear and take that hell of a ride down the slippery slope of self-sabotage, knowing that it's all bottoms-up from there? Or will you jump on that beautiful ride of faith, knowing that it may be some ups and downs, but you'll always be right-side-up? Don't take too long to decide; they're waiting to hear from you.

Cynthia Encinas-Concordia

Dream to Rise LLC

https://www.linkedin.com/in/cynthia-concordia-2b51b8116/
https://Facebook.com/cynthia.concordia
https://www.instagram.com/cynthiaconcordia
www.dreamtorise.info

Retired from the World Bank, I have had the best opportunity—through my life journey, to see the value of making a positive impact on others' lives. Now, as I move to the next chapter of my life as a life coach, I feel the calling to make a difference by inspiring others and creating awareness to empower people to choose the life they would love to live.

With me fulfilling my purpose, I am now leaving my footprints so the young generation may be inspired and continue what we are doing – that is to make an impact in this world. For me, this is real happiness.

I want you to live your dreams and welcome each day full of gratitude, saying, "Life is great!"

HOW I TURNED MYSELF FROM BEING A WORRIER TO BECOMING A LIGHT WARRIOR

By Cynthia Encinas-Concordia

Introduction

LIFE. Such a big word, encompassing so many things from different perspectives. For me, life is an adventure, a journey that lets you experience successes, failures, challenges, and interactions with people from different walks of life. Life is also like a game without rules. It is we who set the rules for ourselves based on what we think makes sense, depending on our situation. There are no best or winning rules; it is up to us to define them. Life is a learning experience. Each interaction with every individual contributes to what we become—whether it's how we perceive life, how we view challenges and failures, how we become visionaries for our own purposes, and, most especially, how we are able to impact others' lives and contribute to creating a better world. Life is a blessing that allows us to experience God's love through others and His creations. Life is not just about seeking achievements and accomplishments. We need to experience challenges and failures as well—that is the exciting part about being alive and living life to the fullest.

I would like to share with you my life's journey and how I overcame challenges and reaped achievements, which led me to become a transformational life coach—not just for me, but for my family as well, most especially for my children, Nathalia (31 years old), married to RJ and a mother to Charlie, and Gabriel (26 years old). It will explain why and how I became the Cynthia that you know. What brought about the new Cynthia?

Each one of us has a light to share with others. The only problem is we tend to keep them to ourselves because we are still determining how others would perceive them. We have that fear, doubt, and worry overpowering our light.

When I experienced my struggles leading to my rock bottom, I asked myself, what would happen to me if I stayed there? What will my life be? Will I be living my life to the fullest? Definitely not! During that time, I had to decide whether to choose light or stay in darkness.

Life Story: Problem

I was married for 23 years and blessed with two children. My marriage was a roller coaster ride. I was subjected to domestic violence, which started when my daughter was only five months old back home in the Philippines. Like many immigrant families, we moved to the USA to provide our children with better opportunities, as well as work on my marriage. However, instead of working towards the marriage that I had aspired for, things turned out much differently. By 2011, my late husband was on two restraining orders (the first in 2005 for 72 hours and the second in 2011 for two years). During that two-year period, I remember constantly telling my children that their father loved them so much. I did not want their relationship with their father to break. I believe that, as humans, we all make mistakes and deserve second chances. And so, I was exhilarated when my children invited him to each of their high school and college graduations.

The worst part came four months after their graduation when he died due to massive cardiac arrest. I remember crying so hard when I saw him in the emergency room because there was still so much conflict to work through, not only in our marriage but also with our whole family. I felt we still had a lot of work to do to get to a place of forgiveness—a place that I now felt we could not know because now he was gone.

For six long and agonizing years, I felt nothing but guilt. I stayed in my own dark world, stopped interacting with my friends, became depressed, and ultimately allowed this to impact my physical, mental, and emotional well-being. I had a huge fear of being judged and rejected by others, especially our mutual friends and his family members. Some of those friends and families even stopped communicating with me and our children after his death. Only my relationship with God kept me going during those dark days of despair. He was my source of strength, my hope, and my light.

When I got to the point where I felt life was no longer worth living, my son shared with me that he wanted to go to the *Culinary Institute of America (CIA)* for a Culinary Arts and Food Studies degree. I had completely forgotten that I still had my son, who needed to attend college! By then, I was a single parent, and so came the next worry—how would I be able to afford it? That was the moment when my perspective shifted: I could not keep allowing the past to decide my future; I had my son's dreams to think about! This new perspective motivated me to ensure that I not only provided for my son but would also work on myself in the process.

My focus became working hard, not just to ensure that he got to attend his school of choice but that he also thrived in and graduated from that school. With this newfound motivation and passion, I also started giving myself attention, putting myself in the priority list of people to care about. I worked out every day and ate healthy and nutritious food. I later found out that taking care of my health and well-being helped to boost my confidence, which led to a healthier relationship with my children and my family. I discovered that my positive behavior was mirrored back to me by the people I interacted with. This allowed me to focus more on other areas in my life, like work.

Gabriel's graduation at CIA.
Left to right: Cynthia, Gabriel, and Nathalia

With this newfound confidence, perseverance, and change in perspective, I was promoted, which increased my salary so significantly as to allow even more blessings into my life. Not only that—God connected me with people who gave me advice and insight into downsizing my living situation, which cut 50% off my mortgage. Then, I looked into applying for grants and scholarships. Can you believe I only paid 20% of my son's first-year tuition? You would not believe all the blessings that continuously came pouring in. By God's overwhelming grace, not only did my son finish his college debt-free, but our little family even had extra money to travel to Barcelona to celebrate his success.

Results: Blessings Overflowing

Can you see how the Lord worked in my life? He did not give me the money itself but sent me connections or people who gave me advice, insight, ideas, and gifts. The Lord took care of my problems.

The Lord showered me with the blessings I needed to manifest my dream. The struggles and pains I experienced made me realize that these are a necessary part of my life's journey toward becoming a new and better person. I became stronger, smarter, more creative, and more resilient. I don't believe that the effect of challenges should be to put us down, to stay stuck in our dark bubble, and live a miserable life. Rather, its effect on us should be that we see the chance to make a change, to pick ourselves up, to find out what our character is and where our strengths lie, and a chance to move forward until we see the light at the end of every tunnel. Remember, we cannot see the beauty of gold without going through the fire. Before the glorious sunrise of Easter Sunday is the darkness of the Lenten season.

Due to my life experiences, I have discovered my WHY, which led me to become a life coach—to help and inspire people to realize that they have the power to manifest their dreams and live the kind of life they love. If I could overcome my challenges and turn the hurdles into stepping stones toward a better future, I am sure that others will be able to do it as well.

Because of what my children and I have gone through, they have discovered their strengths and weaknesses, what they're passionate about, and how they can positively impact other people. I am glad they started early.

My daughter, Nathalia, continues to serve as a volunteer firefighter (for eight years) to honor her dad, because it was a volunteer firefighter who helped revive her dad while driving him to the nearby hospital.

Nathalia (3rd from left) and her co-firefighters in Dale City, Virginia

Gabriel has been passionate about food for so long, which is why he chose to do *Culinary Arts and Food Studies*. He likes to travel and enjoys the beauty of nature; he loves to keep discovering what it is that he would really love to be, to have, to create, and to become. He loves connecting with people, learning their culture, and seeing how he can impact them through food. His experience with 2-and-3-Michelin Star restaurants, in Tulum, Mexico, and Australia, as a farmer and forager, and now a Sous Chef and Program Coordinator, inspired him to do more by educating children and parents about basic farming, food systems and promoting the concept of farm to table. He is advocating sustainability in the food industry.

Gabriel, Sous Chef at Grange in Hill Farm, Vermont.

Cynthia (at extreme right) with kids Gabriel and Nathalia in Barcelona, Spain

Being a mom of two beautiful and inspired children, I came to learn and realize that we should not get stuck in our past experiences, in how we were raised, in the paradigms, in our fears, in the feeling that we are undeserving, and in other limiting beliefs that have been blocking us to move forward towards our dream.

We can create our own dream by design in a more expansive way. We can live in abundance if we want to. The only limits in our life are those we impose on ourselves. We are in control of our own lives.

When you believe in yourself and in what you are capable of and then take action to work on it, you'll be surprised by how much more you can do to make a difference in and for the world. Let us always be that light for others so that others may also spread their light for those who need them.

I can say that I became a light warrior when I chose light despite the doubts and worries which I have nurtured in my thoughts. It was through those dark moments I saw the beauty of the light, which I truly value. You won't be able to appreciate light if you have not gone through darkness. **How do I remain in my power and continue what I do?**

It is my purpose. This keeps me on fire and focused on where I am going. When I created my dream by design and tested my dream, I knew I would be living the life which was prepared for me by God. He is using me as His instrument to spread love and compassion wherever I go. My vision is to spread sunshine and happiness to the people I meet so this may create a ripple effect. I want peace, kindness, compassion, and love to prevail here on earth.

Again, this then led me to: become a life coach, write my book (My Journey Into Becoming), create a mastermind group to help each and every member of the community to manifest their dreams, and launched my podcast so my messages and the stories of my guest speakers will inspire others so later on, they could also be a light warrior themselves.

On top of that, I have also volunteered as a Rotarian at the Rotary Club Pasay EDSA back home in the Philippines to see how I can serve my Filipino brothers who live in poverty.

I also volunteer at Family Services, Fairfax County in Virginia to mentor a 10-year- old child who has been abused by her father.

<u>Gifts Derived from My Challenges</u>

But what I appreciate from what I have gone through in life is that:

- I interrupted the history of domestic abuse within my family and am now leaving a legacy not only to my children and grandchildren but to the people we meet on a daily basis.
- I am now a stronger, improved, creative, resilient, assertive, resourceful, and compassionate person because I am spreading love.
- Now, I'm committed to living my purpose to be a blessing for somebody.
- Now, I'm committed to helping others be the best version of themselves.
- Now, I'm committed and passionate about teaching people that they have the true power within them to live the life they love.

Secrets That Will Impact Your Life

For me, the only secret that will impact our lives is this: We CAN live our lives to the fullest!!! Even with limited time and resources, we have the power to create our dreams and live the life we love. How?

1. Know our WHY or purpose. When we know our mission in life, this will be our living guide. All our plans and actions will be geared toward our dream or mission.

2. Take risks and learn to face fear. If we stay within our comfort zone, we will not discover the opportunities in store for us. Learning is part of growth. When we challenge ourselves, we thrive. Believe in yourself and enjoy the journey!

3. Be grateful for all that we have. The more grateful we are, the more abundantly we see life, and then we will have a growth mindset. Remember, our thoughts are powerful. What we think becomes reality.

4. Learn to forgive. Remember, forgiveness is about us. When we forgive, we become freer, fuller, and experience an abundance of grace. We will have inner peace. Let go of the past, get wisdom from our experience, and move forward.

5. Be a leader, ready to help, that promotes happiness, support, love, compassion, and peace. Have the courage, take that challenge, and make the change!

In my life journey, I have discovered that Jesus came to resurrect my hope, my calling, my faith, my joy, and my life.

Remember, life is a gift for us to share while we still can. Let us continue spreading sunshine and happiness to all!

Katie Tschida

Founder of KRT Virtual Assistant. LLC

https://www.linkedin.com/in/krtvirtualassistant/
www.facebook.com/krtvirtualassistant
www.instagram.com/krtvirtualassistant
www.krtvirtualassistant.com
https://links.krtvirtualassistant.com/

Katie Tschida is a homeschooling mom to 3 kids who, in 2020, decided to take the plunge and become an entrepreneur.

She has since specialized as a digital organizer and accountability assistant, helping business owners tame their overflowing inboxes and meet their goals. With her assistance, business owners can keep a sense of organization and direction in their work.

Katie loves to travel and create memories with her family. She believes that the experiences gained through travel can be a valuable learning opportunity for all.

Katie's mission is to help business owners streamline their processes to maximize their time and energy. With her help, her clients can free up their time to focus on what matters most, achieve their goals, and spend quality time with their families.

HOW TO ESCAPE FROM SELF-SABOTAGE AND FIND SUCCESS

By Katie Tschida

Boots were made for walking. Being the stubborn woman I am, I made sure that my boots did more than walk. I enlisted in the military around the turn of the century. I wanted to make a difference, but I wasn't sure how yet. Before I could choose, I needed to get through basic training, and this first part of my journey was anything but basic for me.

I ended up getting sick but refused to see a doctor. If I missed a day of training, I would be set back. It wasn't until I pushed myself to the point of passing out that I felt like my future would be further from me. Three days of bedrest felt like torture. I kept thinking that I would be behind on my training! I won't graduate! I'm going to miss out on so much because I got sick! I got lucky though. Between the kindness of my superiors and my determination, I was able to graduate from basic training. From there, I continued my journey en route and went off to Military Occupational Specialty (MOS) School.

As I was gearing up for training after arriving at my assigned unit, my superiors contacted me to deliver some unexpected news. I was no longer going to the training I was looking forward to.

"You're being assigned to a unit in California," my superior told me.

Dumbfounded, I replied, "What do you mean? I don't live in California."

"You are being deployed."

"What are you talking about?"

"You're going to Iraq in two to three months."

What about my current unit?"

"You will be with a handful of them, but not all."

"What about my MOS training?" I asked with both concern and frustration.

"You're not doing that anymore. You are going to do something else."

I argued with him on the phone for a few minutes, but ultimately, I knew I would have to go. So I did more training and went off to Iraq as part of a filler unit. We took care of laundry and textiles, and to my surprise, it was fun! Even though I didn't have a rough time in the military, I still dealt with my fair share of negative encounters. These encounters turned me into a rebel. Simply put, if you're a well-liked soldier, you tend to get picked for training that others don't.

Some of it came down to willpower. Some soldiers don't have the determination that others do. And so I did whatever I could to prevent myself from earning any promotions. I didn't want to be in the sergeant rank. It wasn't until my deployment that I experienced fairer treatment. It inspired me to want to step up for people who were in my place.

You have some status after going through several military pieces of training. Yet, you don't have enough status to stand up for others. I wanted to stand up to those who were treating somebody else indifferently. After returning from the deployment, I went after my sergeant rank. Once I accomplished this status, I worked hard to help others. I worked towards giving the lower enlisted their voices so they felt heard. They mattered. They shouldn't be belittled. They need to be treated with respect.

I carried this empowering mindset over to my business. However, the rebel who did what she could to not move up was ever-present. She told me, "People won't listen to you. They will undermine you. They won't give you the time because you don't deserve it."

You can't run a business that way. You can't raise a family that way. You can't be the best version of yourself with that negative thinking.

So I set out to make a change. One of the first things I did was find like-minded business owners to connect with. These people empowered me to keep going. Working with people who care has helped me find ways to express myself and overcome barriers.

My biggest barrier would often put me into self-sabotage mode. This barrier is people-pleasing. People pleasing wore down my confidence and self-esteem. It affected my relationship with my clients. This, in turn, affected my livelihood.

No matter how small a stumble, my subconscious would tell me I couldn't do something. Then, it would convince me why I couldn't do anything else. I could get 10 tasks done in a day, yet still have 10 incomplete tasks on my to-do list.

I invested in a business coach not long after. This coach gave me some hard truths to face; truths I was trying to avoid and roadblocks I would detour from and never fix. I would push back deadlines or miss them altogether.

I had to learn to tolerate discomforts and teach myself self-compassion. It's challenging, but once I did, I found out exactly how I was self-sabotaging and how it led to people pleasing. One is procrastination. I am not a lazy person, yet somehow, I would always find a way to talk myself out of doing things that needed to get done. My procrastination would take me down the path of disorganization, which is ironic.

I help businesses organize their digital clutter! Unfortunately, it was affecting my relationship with others and myself. I would waste time in ways that made me feel productive, but they didn't push me closer to my goals. And this self-sabotage was a cycle. I had to learn to recognize the patterns to gain control of my life.

It started with giving myself grace and understanding. Mistakes happen. Life happens. I am human. Grace evolved into self-discipline. With discipline, I could stop making excuses or finding other things to do. I could finally finish the important tasks that matter! Then came the organization. I learned not to over-schedule myself and make room for failure. Failure is not the end of the journey. It's room for growth. It's a way to walk my stubborn boots down my own path.

Andrea Hunt

Living Deliberately
Transformational Coach

https://www.linkedin.com/company/andrea-hunt-transformational-life-coaching-eft-services/
https://www.facebook.com/livingdeliberatelytoday
https://www.instagram.com/living.deliberately.today/
https://www.dreahunt.com
https://lnk.bio/KDZ7

Andrea Hunt is a world traveling transformational life coach and EFT practitioner for professional expats, digital nomads, and those who are finding the courage to take the big leap abroad.

She helps women thrive abroad in other countries by overcoming sabotaging beliefs and negative self-talk, insecurities, playing it small and staying stuck in old patterns. Using transformational coaching and the mind-body technique called the Emotional Freedom Technique (EFT Tapping), she empowers people to thrive abroad.

BREAKING FREE FROM SELF-SABOTAGE: A GUIDE TO EMOTIONAL REGULATION USING THE EMOTIONAL FREEDOM TECHNIQUE

By Andrea Hunt

One of my favorite quotes is from Brad Yates, who says: Self-sabotage is really just misguided self-love. Even when it might not be helpful. For many of us, that might look like making excuses, blaming, procrastinating, giving up too easily, or not even trying because we're 'doomed to fail' anyway. Sound familiar?

I get my clients unstuck from self-sabotage with this approach:

Step 1: Let's understand why we self-sabotage.

Step 2: Let's find out how to identify it.

Step 3: Let's talk about what it's trying to tell us.

Step 4: Unleash the transformative power of EFT tapping to change your feelings/behavior.

What do I know about self-sabotage? I'll tell you a secret: like everyone, I've had plenty of my own battles with self-doubt and self-sabotage. Today, I'm a transformational life coach and EFT practitioner who's now made stepping out of my comfort zone a continuous habit, even when my confidence feels wobbly. I've moved across the world by myself six times to changing my career and launching my business in another country. You don't need to be Superwoman to get out of your own way.

Thanks to EFT tapping, I've figured it out and can help you too.

What are some reasons we self-sabotage?

Firstly, it's important to understand that our subconscious impulses and emotions drive most of our life decisions, behaviors, and responses.

From what I've seen with my clients, several main emotional mindset blocks can lead us to self-sabotage.

1. **Limiting Beliefs** - Ingrained ideas and narratives from things we heard, saw, learned from our environment, etc. or experienced ourselves firsthand. These beliefs affect what we think the world is like, what we believe is possible, and what we can or cannot do.

2. **Imposter Syndrome** - One of the strongest mindset blocks and creators of self-doubt. Negative self-talk might convince us that we're a fraud, everyone is better, and our success is undeserved.

3. **Fear and Worry** - Strong emotional responses evoked from the thought that everything could go wrong, we could fail, or succeed and not be able to handle it.

How do we know if we're self-sabotaging?

Next, the truth is that most of us don't say to ourselves: I'm going to hold myself back from what I want. We believe in ourselves and push ourselves out of our comfort zones...

And then something funny happens. We stop ourselves.

What are common forms of self-sabotage?

Playing It Safe: When we fear change or security is our top priority, we might keep ourselves back and call it 'being realistic' even when we've outgrown situations/people, etc.

Procrastination: When we put things off because we don't have (make) time. We have all-or-nothing thinking, like: I can't start eating healthy today because I already ate fast food at lunch.

Blame: When we can't succeed because of 'them.' We're too busy, no one helps us, no one wants to see us succeed. It's everyone else's 'fault.'

Perfectionism: When we can't do it 100% perfectly, we don't do it at all. We wait until we're 100% ready. We can't start/finish something because it's not perfect.

Defeatism: When we see things we want and think: 'Why bother trying?' Or we try but then give up easily because we assume it's ruined, too late, or not worth it.

Control: When we try to control it by doing it all ourselves. We may not let others help, so we're exhausted, burned out, and irritated at everyone and everything.

Stuck: When we're in freeze mode because every action or thought has WHAT IFs tied to it. We are too scared to take action.

What to do when you notice self-sabotaging patterns

Firstly, it's important not to beat ourselves up, criticize, or be judgmental. This is the time to be kind, compassionate, and get curious. Ask yourself some gentle questions to understand what the self-sabotaging behavior trying to show you:

What is My Motivation?

Am I driving this intention, or is someone making me? Is this goal/dream driven by my values and purpose, or is it for others? What does it bring me on an emotional level?

What are My Fears?

Identify the fears that are causing a flight or freeze situation. Am I afraid to fail or scared I couldn't handle it if I succeeded? What is the worst that could happen?

Where is My Resistance?

Resistance shows up when we subconsciously rebel against a person or authority figure. Am I rebelling against someone or something from my present or past?

Am I Stuck in All-or-Nothing Thinking?

Do I need to be perfect, 100% ready, or 100% confident? Did I make a mistake and 'ruin' it, so I might as well just accept failure?

Am I Catastrophizing?

Catastrophizing is assuming a worst-case scenario with drastic consequences. Am I worried 'They' will criticize or judge me? Am I afraid of being exposed?

Why should I use EFT tapping for the process?

Lastly, now that we have honestly acknowledged all of our feelings and what's behind our self-sabotage, we can start using the Emotional Freedom Technique (EFT Tapping) to clear the emotions around the issue.

Being able to calm fears or reframe where we're stuck is truly instrumental to moving forward so that we can choose a different response and behaviors to move forward.

- EFT tapping uses your fingers to lightly tap acupuncture points on the face connected to the body's energy system.
- EFT tapping calms the amygdala in the brain responsible for the fight, flight, and freeze responses.
- EFT works to 're-wire' the brain's neural pathways to create different emotional responses.
- EFT tapping works by articulating negative thoughts/ emotions/beliefs to clear the emotional charge.

Do you just need a bit of help to push your dreams forward? My Release, Refresh, Re-create your Life and Mindset program addresses your personalized mindset breakthroughs, releasing mindset blocks and core-sabotaging behaviors. Let me help you get out of your own way!

Sources:

https://www.ncbi.nlm.nih.gov/pmc/articles/PMC6381429/
https://pubmed.ncbi.nlm.nih.gov/36438382/
https://www.thelondoneconomic.com/lifestyle/tapping-therapy-rewires-brains-neural-pathways-reduce-addiction-food-cravings-47429/
https://neurosciencenews.com/tapping-stress-19837/
https://eftuniverse.com/research-studies/

Philippa Scott

Fantastic Futures
Perinatal Therapist

https://www.linkedin.com/in/philippa-scott-6b6a5475/
https://www.facebook.com/fantasticfuturesaustralia/
https://www.instagram.com/fantasticfuturesbirth_beyond/
https://www.fantasticfuture.com.au/

Philippa (Pippa) is an Australian TRTP practitioner, perinatal mental health, and parenting support specialist. Her passion is helping people overcome trauma and achieve emotional wellbeing through TRTP. Drawing on her background as a Doula and childbirth educator, and her lived experience of overcoming trauma, Pippa brings a wealth of knowledge and experience to her practice.

Pippa specializes in perinatal mental health and parenting support, empowering new and expectant parents to build strong and healthy relationships with their children and create fantastic futures for their families.

As a TRTP practitioner, Pippa uses a unique approach to address trauma at its root cause, allowing her clients to release the emotional pain of their past and overcome anxiety, depression, PTSD, and other trauma-related symptoms. Her clients consistently report feeling a sense of peace, clarity, and joy after working with her.

SELF-SABOTAGE FREE FERTILITY

By Philippa Scott

Through my story as a mother of four, perinatal therapist, and Doula, we will delve into the complex issues of subconscious core beliefs, birth trauma, and self-sabotage, and how they can manifest in our relationships with our children. Philippa's journey highlights the challenges of balancing personal healing and parenting and serves as a powerful reminder of the importance of self-reflection and growth in our roles as parents.

Parenthood is a complex and demanding journey that requires patience, resilience, and a willingness to confront one's own limitations. However, for individuals who have experienced trauma ("little t" trauma) or distress, parenting can be particularly challenging, leading to self-sabotaging behaviors that impact conception, pregnancy, birth, and parenting.

My journey of childbirth has been an incredible one, filled with challenges and triumphs. My first birth was a Caesarean, leaving me feeling distressed and unsatisfied. However, I was determined to make my next childbirth experience a positive one, so I embarked on the journey to become a doula.

When it came time for me to give birth again, I opted for a vaginal birth. My second daughter was born, and I felt a sense of accomplishment and pride. However, this was only the beginning of my journey. I had two more daughters at home, and each one taught me something more and had a profound impact on me, both emotionally and spiritually.

Core beliefs are deeply ingrained and fundamental beliefs that individuals hold about themselves, others, and the world around them.

These beliefs are often shaped by personal experiences, cultural and societal values, and family upbringing, and they can have a significant impact on various aspects of an individual's life, including fertility and parenting decisions.

Core beliefs are held in the unconscious mind, meaning that individuals may not be fully aware of them on a conscious level. Despite this lack of awareness, these beliefs can still profoundly impact an individual's thoughts, emotions, and behaviors. The subconscious mind, which operates below the level of conscious awareness, can influence bodily functions such as heart rate, breathing, and even immune response. Likewise, it can impact fertility, pregnancy, birth and postnatal bonding, and breastfeeding. As a result, core beliefs held in the unconscious can ultimately influence physical health and well-being. Becoming more aware of these beliefs and how they impact the subconscious can be important in promoting overall wellness and making positive changes in one's life.

Moreover, it's essential to note that childhood trauma, whether big "T" or little "t," can also impact an individual's core beliefs, which, in turn, can influence their fertility and parenting decisions. Trauma can affect an individual's self-worth, ability to trust others, and ability to form secure attachments, impacting their decision-making and approach to fertility and parenting.

Core beliefs that stem from childhood trauma can lead to self-sabotaging behaviors in the context of fertility and parenting. For example, an individual who believes they are not worthy of having children due to past experiences of trauma may avoid seeking medical treatment or engaging in fertility-enhancing behaviors. Similarly, negative beliefs about oneself or one's ability to parent may lead to behaviors that undermine one's effectiveness as a parent, such as avoiding challenging situations or becoming overly controlling.

Furthermore, negative core beliefs resulting from childhood trauma can impact an individual's parenting style and perpetuate negative behavior patterns. For example, someone who experienced abuse or neglect in childhood may struggle to provide emotional support and guidance to their own child, potentially perpetuating the cycle of abuse or neglect. Or go too far the other way and parent from guilt and fear without healthy boundaries and discipline.

Generational trauma refers to the transmission of trauma from one generation to the next. This can occur when individuals who have experienced trauma pass down their experiences, behaviors, and coping mechanisms to their children and grandchildren. These patterns of behavior can perpetuate a cycle of trauma, impacting subsequent generations' mental and emotional health.

Addressing both core beliefs and childhood and generational trauma through therapy or other forms of support can be instrumental in breaking free from self-sabotaging behaviors and negative patterns of behavior, leading to a more fulfilling and successful family life.

For myself, it took sixteen years of parenting for me to find myself falling completely apart. Don't get me wrong, there were plenty of warning signs along the way. Workaholism, a brain aneurism, and then finally adrenal fatigue. My doctor wanted me to take three months off work to recover, but I couldn't afford to do that. I needed a fast solution that would allow me to continue to work and parent.

I discovered a process called TRTP, and within a month of booking in, I had completed the program and was well on my way to complete healing. The very first session rewrote my limiting and negative subconscious core beliefs, and for the first time, I wasn't parenting out of guilt and fear but love and confidence! I immediately knew that I needed to bring this to parents and parents-to-be. I trained as a TRTP practitioner at the very next opportunity and began using it in my private practice with incredible results.

Uncovering who I was without the negative beliefs I had taken on as a child was life-changing. Don't get me wrong, I had a good childhood in many ways. I knew I was loved, cherished, and believed in, yet despite this, I had taken on ideas about myself and life from my childhood that impacted not only my life choices but my experiences of pregnancy, birth, and my parenting choices.

Parenting from love often involves responding to your child's needs with empathy, understanding, and compassion. It involves creating a safe and nurturing environment for your child to grow and develop in their own unique way. Parenting from love also involves setting boundaries and limits but doing so in a gentle and loving way.

Parenting from fear, on the other hand, can involve reacting to your child's behavior with anxiety or anger and making decisions based on a need for control or a fear of something bad happening. It can also involve being overly protective or limiting your child's experiences out of fear of potential harm or failure.

Breaking the cycles of trauma can be challenging, but it is possible. It requires a commitment to personal growth, self-awareness, and a willingness to break free from negative behavior patterns. By breaking the cycle of trauma, you can create a better future for yourself and your family, and ensure that the trauma of the past does not burden future generations.

Gina Renee

Gina Renee Coaching LLC
Money Mindset/Money Relationship Coach

https://www.facebook.com/gina.renee.144
https://www.instagram.com/alwaysginarenee
Free Facebook Community:
https://www.facebook.com/groups/wealthywomenontherise

Born in NY and living in sunny Arizona, Gina is an Author and Money Mindset/Money Relationship Coach helping women all over the world release their money blocks, heal their money wounds, and transform their financial reality.

Coming from a poor upbringing and spending her adult life living paycheck to paycheck, Gina understands what it's like to constantly worry about money, feeling like there's never enough.

Having done her own healing and transformational work over the last several years to create a financially thriving life, Gina draws from her personal journey, coaching skills, and intuitive abilities to help other women feel safe with money so they can have a lot more of it.

She understands that because of our subconscious programming, we often sabotage our financial abundance and in this book Gina shares how to stop it once and for all so we can create the wealth we truly desire.

NO MORE SABOTAGING YOUR FINANCIAL ABUNDANCE

By Gina Renee

If you want more money, you have to understand why you don't already have it or aren't getting it. When I ask the women in my world what's getting in the way, some will respond with situations and circumstances. But many of them respond with... "Me." Most of us know that the real reason we don't have what we want is because we keep getting in our own way. In other words, we self-sabotage. But most of us don't know why it happens or what to do about it.

This was true for me as well. Money had been hard my whole life. I grew up a poor kid, and as an adult, I lived paycheck to paycheck no matter how much or how hard I worked, with a frequently negative bank account. I decided that enough was enough. I was ready for more money, extra money, and I started taking action. When the money finally showed up very easily and faster than ever before, just like I had been working for... I self-sabotaged. I was in the beginning stages of my coaching business, still working my 9-5 and trying to build a business on the side. I decided I wanted to make six figures per year doing this life-changing work and had been trying for quite a while. One afternoon I got an idea for a new program. I put up one post about it and made a little over $1100 in less than an hour. This might not seem like much money to you, but it was more money than I was making in a week at a job where I was working really freakin' hard, and it was the fastest, easiest money I had ever made, dropped into my account for work I hadn't even done. And I panicked. This should have been a moment of celebration. I got exactly what I had desired for so long, and yet here I was, crippled with discomfort that consumed my entire body. I was the woman who could barely pay her bills, always having more month at the end of my money, and in 60 minutes, everything just changed. This was too much, too easy, and somehow felt wrong.

I'd love to tell you that at that moment, I knew exactly what was happening, that I avoided self-sabotage and went on to create hundreds of thousands of dollars with this program. Not quite. I'll tell you what happened, but first I must let you know that it's not always this dramatic. Sometimes it's a bit more subtle, harder to recognize, and looks like the car breaking down, a family member needing something, or some other unexpected expense coming up every time you have just a bit more money.

And you might be wondering why. When we really want more money, and having just enough for our needs with nothing left over feels so bad, and having extra would only make things better, why do we still self-sabotage?

Because we are protecting ourselves.

This is the way we are wired. Most people think that we only protect ourselves from something bad, so when the outcome is perceived as good, this won't happen. But the truth is, we protect ourselves from the unknown. From what's unfamiliar. Bad or good. Our subconscious is designed to keep us the same because same is safe. When it comes to money, there is a certain amount that is beyond what's familiar or feels safe for you, so when you get close to that number or reach it, you will feel uncomfortable. This is where you stop taking action, you stop doing what's working, or you get the money and lose it. But you don't have to. You can overcome self-sabotage just like I did and go on to create a life of financial abundance and overflow with ease.

And here's how:

For starters, understand that this is a normal process. Expect that it will happen when you make a change in your life, even if that change is good. Remember: Our subconscious mind sees the unfamiliar as unsafe.

- Identify your money beliefs and what amount feels safe for you. Knowing this allows you to change your beliefs and expand to safety with bigger numbers.
- Recognize self-sabotage when it starts to occur and have some empowering, go-to beliefs to anchor into so you can stop it or reverse it quickly.
- Be aware of your patterns so you can disrupt them.
- Get comfortable sitting with and holding your uncomfortable emotions.
- Know that nothing is wrong and you are safe. Remember, it all comes down to safety.
- And have a coach or mentor to guide you. Sometimes we just can't see it for ourselves or navigate our way through it.

Today my financial reality looks very different. I never went on to sell that program again, and I haven't made six figures in my business. Yet. But I have reached six figures with all sources combined. I have coached many incredible women and still do. I no longer live paycheck to paycheck. All bills are paid with lots of money left over. My bank accounts are flourishing. I've expanded the amounts I'm able to receive with ease well beyond that $1000. And when an amount of money comes in "too fast" or feels like "too much," I'm prepared. I know exactly what to do. I receive it all without self-sabotaging.

And I do this by practicing exactly what I've shared with you in this chapter.

Change feels uncomfortable. Growth feels uncomfortable. More money than you're used to will feel uncomfortable. Self-sabotage happens to avoid all of this. So when you know in advance that you are safe, learn to hold the discomfort, and then navigate through it, you'll get to the other side every time. You'll never self-sabotage again, and the financial abundance you desire will be yours.

Carol Bustamante

Carol Bustamante
Psychic Intuitive Light Coach

https://www.facebook.comcarol.beckerbustamante
https://www.instagram.com/Intuition_0f_Light/
www.carolbustamante.com

Hello people of the Universe and Welcome to my energy! My name is Carol Bustamante and I am a Psychic Intuitive Light Coach and an Integrated Energy Therapist. My passion is helping people see their own worth and the love that they already are.(how do i know, I was there @ rock bottom) I guide people back into their light and wholeness. So they can go and live their lives with a new found passion and insight. My readings are warm and accurate. My Integrated Energy session gets the "Issues out of the tissues" and I use Solfeggio frequencies (sound healing) Everything is energy and frequency.

My Mantra : I am love made manifest, I have come to awaken this in you all

- Lady Sarah

TURNING MY PAIN INTO POWER & PURPOSE

By Carol Bustamante

Hello people of the universe, and welcome to my energy! My name is Carol Bustamante, and I'm sharing with you my story about how I overcame self-sabotage. But first let me give you a glimmer into my life so you can understand the dynamics of the energy I was born into.

My dad was a United States marine, and after his service to his country, he worked for the United States Postal Service. My mother was a well-educated woman. She graduated from mount Saint Vincent's in New York, and after her graduation she worked in New York City. They met and got married and wanted to start a family. Year after year, they tried to get pregnant, but it just wasn't happening. If I remember correctly, my mother told me that her doctor told her to look into adoption, and it was highly unlikely she would ever get pregnant. My mother had such a desire to have a family they finally decided to adopt children. My parents went through their Catholic Church to seek out adoption agencies. It took some time to find, but they found one in Canada. And finally, my parents were about to be living their dream. They received a phone call that their baby boy was ready to be picked up. They got in their Chevrolet and drove off to Canada to pick up my brother. While she was at the orphanage, she put in a request for a baby girl, and then the nuns told her they would contact her. Fast forward five years later and my mother got a call that they had a baby girl (that's me) ready for them, and off to Canada they went. A year and a half go by, and my mother gets another call. They have another baby boy up for adoption, and off they left for Canada. That was their last trip. My parents had their family, and it was all finally flowing.

A few years later, my mom wasn't feeling great, so she made a doctor's appointment to find out what was going on with her health. She thought she was going through menopause, and lo and behold, after a few tests, the doctor told my mother that she was pregnant at 42. Back then, it wasn't normal to be pregnant at that age. Most moms were about 25 to 30 and were all done having kids. I remember my mom being so happy to actually feel a life growing inside her, and at one point, I'm not sure what my father was thinking, but he just went with the flow. Their friends were very happy for them. It was a miracle.

My parents were good-hearted people, they lived a simple life, and they loved us. Back then, people were a product of their time period. Men were the ones who went to work, and the mothers stayed home taking care of the children. If you couldn't afford things, you just didn't buy them. When dad came home, he made himself a cocktail, and my mother would smoke her cigarettes while making dinner. It was just like today's parents, except they come home and spark up with marijuana and crack open a white claw. No judgment here, just observation. Back then, time started to move faster, and everything was changing except my parents' mindset. It felt like they were stuck in an old way of thinking and outdated programming. At least, that's how I saw it. I feel like most families were like us; many dads cracked open a beer and most mothers smoked their cigarettes. That was their outlet in a way, and it was how they dealt with life.

I'm fast forwarding to my Catholic grammar school days, when I was exposed to music, arts, and prayer. I was always singing or humming. Most teachers were Franciscan nuns, and of course, we were always around priests. We started our day with prayer and the Pledge of Allegiance. I remember my class was small, and everyone knew each other. Even the parents were tight- knit. Most parents watched out for other children back then. I usually walked to school with my brothers, but once when I was in second grade, I walked home alone. Oh, how times have changed. Back then, I knew I felt what a true community was. I always felt safe and supported by my teachers and school. I was very creative, and my spirit was intense and loud. I was a tomboy, and I didn't really know anything else. I wanted to follow in my older brothers' footsteps and go to Paramus Catholic High. My grades weren't good enough, and neither was my attitude. So, my parents decided to send me to a public high school. Reflecting on this, I am laughing now. I had no idea what was before me. I was a strong-willed girl with a song in her heart and could also kick your ass if you stepped out of line with my friends. I was always about truth, and I tried to do what the right thing was. I guess it's that good Catholic upbringing and watching my mother being an honest, strong, and good God-loving person.

My high school years were fun for the most part. I loved socializing and having fun. I was always doing something creative and making people laugh. My grades weren't great, along with my attitude, like I said before, and I was in the principal's office from time to time. There was a part of me that didn't care to learn what they were teaching. None of it resonated with me, so I decided to make the best of it and joined the choir, art, basketball, softball, volleyball, which was my favorite. I was proud to be co-captain of the volleyball team. I remember I wore Sergio Valente and Gloria Vanderbilt jeans, size 14. And yes, I was slightly chubby. Those were the days when we thought we were fat. In the 80s, the trend was to have big hair, a thin waist, big boobs, long designer nails, and tan skin. And the makeup I wore back then was Rocky Horror meets Boy George, so it was creative and liked attention. Oh, my goodness! I'm laughing at myself, reminiscing all the awful styles back then and what I did to myself. I'm surprised we all didn't get asphyxiated by the Aqua Net hairspray we used to make our hair really big. And how about that Maybelline black eyeliner that we used to light with a BIC lighter so the product would go smooth on our eyes? Ah, the good old days.

I started feeling like I didn't know what wanted to do for the rest of my life. I knew I loved art, singing, and being creative. I decided to go to Bergen Community. I graduated from Bogota High School back in 1986, and went to college for theater and joined the volleyball team. For a while, it worked out until I found it boring, and my soul wasn't fulfilled. I finally dropped out of Bergen and decided to go to Parisian Beauty Academy (oh my dear mother, God rest her soul. I was a handful at that age) and to earn my cosmetology license. It was the right choice. I felt it in my heart. I was learning everything about hair, skin, and nails.

The teachers were good, especially Miss Clair. She was one tough personality and an excellent teacher. She loved teaching. You always knew where you stood with her. If you disrespected her, she would address you right in front of the class, and she didn't give a rat's ass (a term we used back in the day) if she hurt your feelings. She was no joke, and I admired her for that. It was her strength and honesty that shined brightly. She was always on point, and she truly cared about people. Looking back in reflection while I am typing this, I realize it was a trait I would continue to seek in people. Reflecting on my life at that time, something clicked within my soul. I started looking at everyone differently in a deeper way. Wow, did that open my eyes to what people are capable of. The rose-colored glasses were slowly coming off, and my mindset started to change. And speaking of change, *I* was changing, and I wasn't sure if it was for the better. I felt like I was lost, even with my strong attitude, and I'll kick your ass if you mess with me vibe. Remember, I grew up with three brothers, and my masculine side was dominant. I grew into my femininity years later.

I got married at 26 (208lbs.) and had my first child at 28. I had my last child at 35. I got even heavier after my second son was born. I was 240 lbs. (I was on six different medications, and I needed a sleep apnea machine to help me breathe) and growing oppressed. I put everyone else before myself. How was that working for me? It wasn't! I was hard on myself, and I was in denial about how I dealt with life, with food being my drug of choice. Although at the time, I didn't see it that way. Until one day, out of the blue, I was spending time with my cousin on my husband's side. She was someone I looked up to and admired. She had a beautiful way about her and how she delivered the truth. She pulled me aside and asked if I had taken a good look in the mirror. I replied to her as if maybe I had a stain on my clothes. She continued telling me I was a beautiful woman and that my children were adorable. She asked me, "Don't you want to see your children grow up? She was my mirror with love and truth. She said if you continue down this road, I am afraid your children will be motherless. It's not healthy the weight you carry, she told me. I was 5'5" at size 4X with a 53-inch waist, and apple-shaped as well. I was using a sleep apnea machine with the onset of diabetes and high blood pressure! I felt her pain and concern for me, and it all hit me like a ton of bricks. I almost couldn't take a breath. Later that day, I was on my knees in emotional pain. I was sobbing over all the what ifs and crying over the emotional pain I was experiencing within myself.

This is where my journey to overcoming self-sabotage began. The same day, I started researching everything diet and health-related. I stumbled on an ad for weight loss surgery. Back then, they offered the lap band or the Roux, NY gastric bypass surgery. Something felt right about the gastric bypass, so I researched it even further. I questioned everyone who underwent the surgery and made my own decision. My husband at the time agreed with me. He just wanted me to be healthy. I knew what I needed to do. It didn't matter what my family said about it, I was going all in. I knew it wasn't just food-related; it was my emotional state and how I realized I was in self-sabotage mode, and I needed to see the light. My cousin Lozita was my light in the darkness. This was the moment I knew what I needed to do. I took a long deep inner look, and I said to myself no more!

During my research, I came across an obesity help forum. This was a group of people that went through the surgery. I found a lot of excellent reviews on Dr. Capella. He was "the" doctor to go to. He had created a different version of the gastric bypass by adding a band around the stoma so it wouldn't stretch out. I felt good about choosing him, but I also wanted to know if I was making the right choice. It's amazing how the Universe conspires with you when you align with your purpose. One day, I met my cousin's girlfriend. She had the exact same surgery I was researching by the SAME doctor I was looking into. It was a huge sign to me. After that, I called his office to make an appointment, and the rest just fell into place. I knew I had a lot of work ahead of me, Physically and emotionally. He offered me the chance to join a group of people who already had the surgery, along with newbies as well. I wanted to be a part of it all, 100%. This group helped me so much by preparing me mentally, and I learned from their wisdom. I made a vow to myself (and my children) that I would not return to my old behaviors, so I leaned into self-help books, videos, and therapy groups to unlearn my old ways. It was the toughest thing I had ever gone through in my life!!! The part of the illusion I was holding was "It's just food," and not looking at it was all self-created by my ego, emotional wounds, lack of self-love, and negative self-talk. Wow!

I had the surgery, and it went well. I had no complications. I followed the doctor's orders to the T! I only drank protein shakes for the first four weeks after the operation. I slowly integrated soft food while going to group to get better physically, but emotionally I was still vomiting up so much old pain, self-loathing, and dark energy. I was in a rebirth. This was the beginning of overcoming self-sabotage. I am in my 50s now, and I maintain a healthy weight at 120 lbs. and a size four. And I have a healthy mindset. I treat myself with love and am my own caregiver. I learned to nurture myself. The best wisdom I have gained is that the most important relationship I needed to be in was with myself. I learned to release the power of my ego that caused power struggles within my heart and let go of the fears that overwhelmed me. I opened my heart to the divine truth, and I let go of my own limiting beliefs. The greatest gift I've learned is to love all parts of myself and that I am already whole. It's all working out just beautifully. I love the life I created with a healthy mindset and taking one day at a time, living in conscious awareness and gratitude for everyone and everything in my life. I transmuted my pain and suffering into self-love, joy, and contentment. My new mantra: I am love made manifest. I have come to awaken this in you all.

Sarah-Jane Layton

Soul Freedom
Soul Healer

https://www.linkedin.com/in/sarah-janelayton/
https://www.facebook.com/sarecare
https://www.instagram.com/sarahjane_layton/
https://www.facebook.com/sarahsoulfreedom
https://www.facebook.com/groups/1917204821989604/?ref=share

Sarah-Jane Layton is a Mother, Soul Healer and Coach, 2 x International Best Selling Author and Mumpreneur as a High Ticket Affiliate Marketer.

She lives an integrous life, creating family and freedom though spirituality, true health and an abundant online business vehicle.

Sarah-Jane empowers new mothers on their spiritual and physical journey to live a happy and healthy life by creating love, peace and harmony for them, their babies and families.

In 2010 she became a Tao Hands Practitioner and loves to empower women, women in business and mothers to breakthrough limiting beliefs to live a life they love!

Sarah-Jane is passionate about empowering people to heal their relationship with money and business, and shares soul knowledge, wisdom and practical techniques to create unlimited abundance.

She also supports women to be financially independent by starting their own soul aligned business.

RELEASE THE RESISTANCE OF YOUR MIND. BREATHE INTO YOUR HEART AND SOUL. YOUR AUTHENTIC VOICE MATTERS.

By Sarah-Jane Layton

Let go of all resistance in your life, anything that challenges you, that you avoid, are in denial about, anything that you wish to put aside because you have strong emotions or thoughts about, you must face it and have the uncomfortable conversations to release your heart and soul.

Embrace it and love it all.

One thing that I've had to do on my journey is come back into integrity with myself. This has involved dealing with things that I've said I was going to do but haven't and clearing this up.

Having conversations that are needed to resolve this and bringing my power back so that I can be the most powerful human being in my reality.

Living an integrous life involves discipline and taking responsibility for your life and what is happening in your life.

I had a personal experience when I committed to showing up online for myself and my business.

I committed to a 90 day gratitude challenge to take myself on, to practice consistently showing up online for 90 days sharing a video of what I'm grateful for every day and why.

This seemed a simple exercise, however, I was challenged on several occasions and found myself engaging and disengaging with this practice.

The benefits of this practice for me were feeling joy and gratitude in my heart, and receiving the unlimited abundance our world has to offer.

It allowed me to focus on everything that I have in my life which was extremely powerful, however sharing this with others got me overthinking a lot, and I got distracted with other things and then stopping sharing and I disappeared from the conversation.

I lost my power and I knew and understood this, however, I continued staying quiet for a couple of months pondering about this, realising that I felt small and powerless as a human being.

I then shared authentically about what had happened and where I was on my journey with a new loving friend Marie who challenged me to show up and I got the courage to share with love and compassion for myself, instead of resistance.

I know that my life is about connecting with my heart and soul and sharing my authentic voice, and my messages to help uplift and serve others so that they can be happier and healthier.

I had to take my power back and stop playing small.

When I get upset or triggered by someone's actions, I now let it go as I can only focus on myself and what I can control, rather than reacting and giving my energy away.

I'd rather use that energy to help me move forward and express myself authentically.

Trust is the key, trust in myself and all the souls that I believe in that have my back, the Divine, Tao, Source, Heaven and Mother Earth, the sun and the moon and countless planets, stars, galaxies, and universes, my spiritual guides, and teachers.

I connect with all of them and invite them to be with me, to love and support me, to help me move forward.

Is best to stop thinking and instead find my power within.

I focus on my lower abdomen, close my eyes, and take some deep breaths inhaling through my nose and out of my mouth.

When I feel stuck and not sure what to do I ask my soul aloud what to do. I then do my soul language and receive the message. I trust the message and take action on my message.

This is what I do to help me move forward on my journey. I surrender to my heart and soul and ask my mind to take a holiday so that I can receive a pure message of love and light, which empowers me and keeps me strong.

Wherever you are on your journey love yourself, honour yourself, appreciate yourself, have compassion for yourself and your journey, and know that everything is happening for you so that you can live a powerful reality that you desire.

Whatever you desire in your life you can have it, I believe in you.

You have the power within to live the life of your dreams if you believe in yourself, are fearless, and take action to change any of your beliefs that are not serving you.

Say affirmations aloud every day to yourself, write them, and believe them.

Create affirmations that serve your highest potential and embody them.

You have all of my love and support to live your wildest dreams and to create the greatest service, unconditional service to all souls and when you can achieve this you will receive unlimited abundance.

I Love you.

It is essential to overcome self-sabotage, to do the inner work, and become the best version of yourself.

Here are some ways that I have incorporated practices and tools into my life, to assist me to move forward.

1. Forgiveness practice – forgive all souls I have hurt or harmed and forgive those that have hurt or harmed me, and forgive myself and my ancestors for the mistakes we've made.
2. Gratitude - write 10 things you're grateful for each morning and evening and why?
3. Journal - Write down what is on your mind and come back into alignment with your true self.
4. Affirmations - Find a power pose and say your affirmations out loud and believe them with every fibre of your being.
5. Limited beliefs - Ask your soul what limiting belief is holding you back and then create an empowering belief.
6. Connect with your soul, the soul of your finances and business, and ask for guidance and wisdom. Never ask the question if you are not prepared to take the action.
7. Exercise for 1/2 hour per day to connect and move your body.
8. Meditation – connect with your vision daily and get excited.

Clear your energy at the start and end of your day.

JOIN THE MOVEMENT!
#BAUW

Becoming An Unstoppable Woman
With She Rises Studios

She Rises Studios was founded by Hanna Olivas and Adriana Luna Carlos, the mother-daughter duo, in mid-2020 as they saw a need to help empower women around the world. They are the podcast hosts of the *She Rises Studios Podcast* as well as Amazon best-selling authors and motivational speakers who travel the world. Hanna and Adriana are the movement creators of #BAUW - Becoming An Unstoppable Woman: The movement has been created to universally impact women of all ages, at whatever stage of life, to overcome insecurities, and adversities, and develop an unstoppable mindset. She Rises Studios educates, celebrates, and empowers women globally.

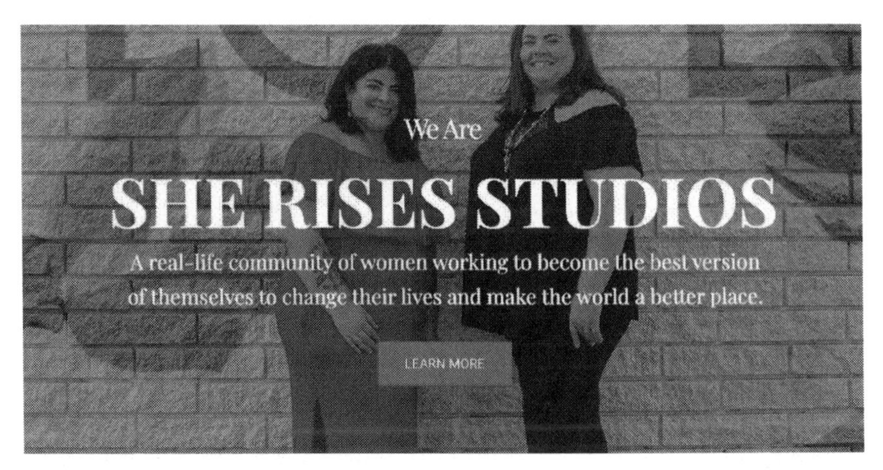

Looking to Join Us in our Next Anthology or Publish YOUR Own?

She Rises Studios Publishing offers full-service publishing, marketing, book tour, and campaign services. For more information, contact info@sherisesstudios.com

We are always looking for women who want to share their stories and expertise and feature their businesses on our podcasts, in our books, and in our magazines.

SEE WHAT WE DO

OUR PODCAST

OUR BOOKS

OUR SERVICES

Be featured in the Becoming An Unstoppable Woman magazine, published in 13 countries and sold in all major retailers. Get the visibility you need to LEVEL UP in your business!

Have your own TV show streamed across major platforms like Roku TV, Amazon Fire Stick, Apple TV and more!

Learn to leverage your expertise. Build your online presence and grow your audience with Fenix TV.
https://fenixtv.sherisesstudios.com/

Visit www.SheRisesStudios.com to see how YOU can join the #BAUW movement and help your community to achieve the UNSTOPPABLE mindset.

Have you checked out the ***She Rises Studios Podcast?***

Find us on all MAJOR platforms: Spotify, IHeartRadio, Apple Podcasts, Google Podcasts, etc.

Looking to become a sponsor or build a partnership?

Email us at info@sherisesstudios.com

Made in the USA
Columbia, SC
02 June 2023

17309698R00050